Across the Hall, Around the World

Teambuilding Tips for Distributed Businesses

Claire Sookman & Susan Garms

First Edition

Multi-Media))
Publications Inc.
Oshawa, Ontario

Across the Hall, Around the World:
Teambuilding Tips for Distributed Businesses
by Claire Sookman & Susan Garms

Managing Editor:	Kevin Aguanno
Copy Editor:	Peggy LeTrent
Typesetting:	Peggy LeTrent
Cover Design:	Troy O'Brien

Published by:
Multi-Media Publications Inc.
Box 58043, Rosslynn RPO
Oshawa, ON, Canada, L1J 8L6

http://www.mmpubs.com/

The graphics used in this book are available from the publisher via download at www.mmpubs.com/catalog

Copyright © 2010 by Multi-Media Publications Inc.

Paperback	ISBN-10: 1554890608	ISBN-13: 9781554890606
Adobe PDF ebook	ISBN-10: 1554890616	ISBN-13: 9781554890613

Published in Canada.

CIP data available from the publisher.

Table of Contents

Acknowledgements

This book is dedicated to the people who have supported us unconditionally.

I would like to thank Josh, my incredible nephew who kept encouraging me to write this book. Thanks so much Josh! Sam, the other love of my life who without your joy and loving spirit this book would not have been possible for me to write and lastly to my mother and father who have passed away. You made me who I am today. Thank you.

Claire

I would like to dedicate this book to my son, Eric, who is the center of my universe and the reason I became a virtual work specialist. Love you!

Susan/Mom

We love you all!

Preamble

So you have decided to create a virtual team. Congratulations!

Now what? Well, as you know, creating virtual teams is not challenge-free. Why? Imagine trying to work and communicate effectively with people whom you may have never met face-to-face and whose personalities you are not familiar with. If this hurdle is not overcome, establishing successful virtual teams can be extremely frustrating. So how do we bridge the virtual distance?

The first step in bridging the distance is to identify the team members on all ends of the technology connection. The second step is to provide your teams with a way to relate with each other. Building relationships is especially critical for effective virtual teams. The foundation of virtual teams is communication and collaboration tools. The hardware is out there and people are getting very productive using them. But who's teaching them about communication skills? To take virtual teams to the next level understanding the behaviour of people on your team and their cultural makeup becomes even more critical in the virtual world. But it doesn't stop there. Working in a virtual environment requires knowing how to build trusting relationships, manage effective virtual meetings, and establish a cohesive team. Result: powerful collaboration, team synergy and performance excellence. This book will give you and your virtual teams the tools to build relationships even though you may be thousands of miles apart from each other. Whether you are a newly-formed team or a high-performing existing team, this book will help you cultivate team effectiveness and collaboration, the hallmarks of an effective virtual team.

In a virtual world, communication is key. Tailoring your approach can spell the difference between a powerful virtual team or a virtual disaster.

CHAPTER 1

Determining and Adapting to DiSC Styles

What is the DiSC Behavioural Profile instrument?

The DiSC instrument helps teams look at how their members tend to behave and what motivates them in any given situation. It breaks behaviours into four categories corresponding to the letters D (Dominance), i (Influence), S (Steadiness) and C (Conscientiousness).

Many of the exercises in this book require that your team complete the DiSC assessment. We suggest you begin by having all your team members complete the assessment. This will help your team understand the most effective way of working with each other.

Behaviour Profile

Instructions

On the following page you will find phrases. How well does each one describe how you are feeling and behaving in a *work situation* on which you are focusing?

- Select the number from 1 to 5 that best indicates how accurately or inaccurately each phrase describes your feelings, thoughts and behaviour in this situation.

- Write the number in the box following the phrase.

- Be sure to respond to every phrase.

- It is very important to use the full range of numbers-1, 2, 3, 4 or 5. The value-to you-of your responses is directly related to how precisely you can weight each response.

- Your first response to the phrase will be the most accurate one. Go with your gut response. This is a case in which first impressions are best.

- You may think at first that some statements don't apply, but the instrument is designed so that the phrases are related in some way to almost every situation. Be sure to respond to each one.

Directions

Working across the four columns, write after each phrase, the number that best describes you in this situation.

    1 = very inaccurate, or does not apply, 2 = inaccurate
    3 = neither accurate or inaccurate, 4 = accurate,
    5 = very accurate

Column 1	Column 2	Column 3	Column 4
Good listener	Want to make the rules	Likes to do things accurately	Wide variety of friends
Put up with things I don't like	Go straight ahead with projects	Like doing things the right way	Liked by others
Willing to follow orders	Act in a forceful way	Do things right the first time	Like to meet people
Will go along with others	Want to win	Think of what makes sense	Fun to be with
Think of others before I decide	Will be the first to act	Like to be precise	See things positively
Willing to help	Do not give in	Shy with others	Feel contented
Understand others' feelings	People see me as powerful	Good at analyzing things	Happy and carefree
Nice to other people	Sure of myself	Think things through	Liven things up
Have warm feelings for people	Want to be in charge	Keep things to myself	Feel relaxed most of the time
Let others lead	Like to take action	Think things over carefully	Happy most of the time
Don't like to cause problems	Quick to act	Don't like too much attention	Find it easy to meet strangers
Don't make demands of people	Feel strong	Don't say much in a group	Communicate in a lively manner
Total column 1	**Total column 2**	**Total column 3**	**Total column 4**
Subtract -1	Add +2	+0	Subtract -2
Score	Score	Score	Score

11

Scoring Directions

Add up the scores in each column, if you haven't done so already, adjust the scores by adding or subtracting as shown, and you'll have your scores for each dimension.

Total column 1_____ = Steadiness

Total column 2_____ = Dominance

Total column 3_____ = Conscientiousness

Total column 4_____ = Influence

Why these particular phrases? The phrases in the DiSC tool have come from ongoing research, and their meaning has been validated and fine-tuned many times, using a broad sample of people of all ages and backgrounds, in a wide variety of situations, and in a range of businesses and professions.

Why the DiSC?

Why the DiSC? The DiSC instrument has been used by twenty million people worldwide, over the past twenty years and it crosses all cultural boundaries. It not only helps teams identify their strengths and challenges they bring to the team, but it teaches them how to adapt their styles to those around them. Through the use of the DiSC, we now have an idea of the behaviour of our team members.

But how do we bring these very diverse personalities together? Before we do that, let's take a moment and talk about why we would need to work on all that human stuff.

In the last few years, we have had an increasing number of requests to help organizations build stronger virtual teams. We hear the same frustration over and over again, "We have great people on our team but why can't they get along better?" The key to creating a strong team is to harness the power of differences. You have heard it before, each individual is unique. Ponder the implications to virtual team success. Each of us brings strengths and challenges to the table. The key to appreciating the unique quality of others is to avoid falling into the trap of believing everyone thinks or enjoys the same things as you do.

Think about your team for a moment; it is likely comprised of a combination of the following four types of "characters" as defined by DiSC:

1. The "Challenging Ones" are represented by the letter "D" (for Dominance) in DiSC, They are the people who like to have control and are inclined to be very direct.

2. Next in your cast of characters are the "Social Butterflies" represented by the letter "i" (for Influence). They are the ones who are extremely friendly, outgoing and communicative. You know, the team builders.

3. Your third group are "The Trusted Ones", represented by the letter "S" (for Steadiness). They are the ones who are always ready and willing to help. You can count on their loyalty and cooperation.

4. To complete the list are "The Analyzers" represented by the letter "C" (for Conscientiousness). They are very demanding on themselves and others. They are sticklers for details and would rather do things right than do things fast.

Throughout the book, you will find exercises that relate back to the DiSC. These exercises will help your team identify and adapt to people's styles with only virtual cues.

Across the Hall, Around the World

Exercises

Across the Hall, Around the World

Adapt to Me

Purpose

The goal of this exercise is to help people adapt to others while on a Teleconference and/or Web conference.

Time/duration

15 minutes

Group size

10 people

Modality

Web conference - whiteboard

Materials

DiSC grid shown below

Process

1. Prior to the meeting create a grid on the whiteboard. The grid should consist of four squares-each square should depict one of the four D,i,S,C styles (see sample below).

2. Ask the team members to brainstorm in chat how to adapt to each style via web conference and/or teleconference.

3. Have the facilitator transcribe the chat onto the whiteboard. Alternatively, have the participants write their answers onto the whiteboard.

Possible answers could include:

- o **Dominance**
  - Come prepared
  - Stick to business
  - Be clear and to the point
- o **Influence**
  - Allow time for socializing
  - Ask for their input
  - Provide them opportunities to be creative
- o **Steadiness**
  - Give them time to make decisions
  - Ask specific question
  - Be personal
- o **Conscientiousness**
  - Present specifics
  - Create an action plan
  - Give them enough information to allow them to make an informed decision.

Debriefing questions

- What do you now know about identifying DiSC styles that you did not know before?
- How will you use this exercise to help you communicate with different styles?

What Is The Most Effective Way To Adapt To Each Style
Via Web Conference

Dominance	influence
Steadiness	Conscientiousness

Determining DiSC Styles - Part 1

Purpose

To generate a list of questions that will be used to determine the DiSC style of someone who has not taken the DiSC assessment.

Occasions arise in which the team will be working with people who have not taken the assessment. These questions will help the team quickly determine the behavioural style of those people to enable them to work more effectively with them.

Time/duration

50 minutes:

- Five minutes for instructions
- 15 minutes for the activity
- 10 minutes for presentation
- 10 minutes for debrief
- 10 minutes to get in and out of break out rooms

Group size

15 people

Modality

Break out rooms (some teleconference and web conference suppliers have the ability to provide participants with break-out rooms where smaller groups within the whole group can work together and then come back together).

Materials

DiSC behavioural assessment

Process

Pre-requisite – everyone on the team must have:

1. Taken the DiSC behavioural assessment
2. Reviewed the characteristics of each DiSC style

Instructions

1. Divide the team into four groups.

2. Assign a DiSC style to each group.

3. Have each group create questions to uncover the DiSC style assigned to them. For example:

   - What did you do this weekend?

   - How is your week going?

   - Tell me what you're working on.

4. Send the groups to their break out rooms.

5. Bring people back into the main room.

6. Have each group shares their list of questions with the other groups.

7. White board the list of questions.

Debriefing questions

- What did you notice about the questions created by the groups?

- How do these questions help you determine people's DiSC styles?

- What might hold you back from using these questions?

Variation

Ask participants to create a list of questions to help them determine someone's style (three minutes).

Determining DiSC Styles – Part 2

Purpose

To interpret the answers to the questions created in Part 1 of Determining DiSC styles.

Time/duration

20 minutes

Group size

15 people

Modality

Web conference – whiteboard

Materials

DiSC grid shown below

Process

1. Prior to the session create a grid, as shown below with the questions they created in part one of the exercise.

2. Ask the team members to write on the whiteboard how each style might answer that question.

3. When debriefing the exercise focus the participant's attention to the following items. Was the answer:

   - Pace: slow vs. fast?

   - Content: detailed or not?

   - Words used: descriptive vs. abrupt?

Example: "What did you do this weekend?"

- o **Dominance**
  - Short and to the point
  - Minimal details
  - Fast and to the point
  - Could sound abrupt to other styles
  - Not people oriented

Possible response: "I was busy all weekend."

- o **Influence**
  - People oriented
  - Likely to be very animated
  - Minimal details – high level overview
  - More focused on the "who" rather than the "what"

Possible response: "We spent the weekend with family and friends and let me tell you how much fun we had…"

- o **Steadiness**
  - Is slow, thoughtful, and deliberate in responding
  - Generally uses feeling words
  - More focused on the "who" rather than the "what"

Possible response: "We went to see houses this weekend but I'm really unsure what to buy. I need to spend some time thinking about it. You know, I really hate pushy real estate agents. They make me feel really uncomfortable."

- o **Conscientiousness**
  - Very task oriented
  - Detail oriented
  - Not focused on people

Possible response: "We are looking for a car so we spent the weekend on the internet searching through all the websites and doing a comparative analysis."

Debriefing questions

• What do you now know about recognizing DiSC styles that you didn't know before?

• How will you use this exercise?

• What might hold you back from using this exercise?

Identifying DiSC Styles

What did you do this weekend?	How has your week been going?
D I S C	D I S C
What are you working on? D I S C	**What are you doing for your vacation?** D I S C

Flexercise

Purpose

The goal of this exercise is to help people identify others style with only virtual cues while on a web conference.

Time/duration

15 minutes

Group size

10 people

Modality

Web conference - whiteboard

Materials

PowerPoint slides

Process

1. Prior to the meeting create a grid on the whiteboard. The grid should consist of four squares-each square should depict one of the four D,i,S,C styles (see sample below).

2. Ask the team members to brainstorm in chat how to identify each style via Web conference and/or teleconference. Have the facilitator transcribe the chat onto the whiteboard.

3. Possible answers may include:

    o **Dominance**

        • Will multi-task

- Will tend to have a powerful voice
- Will give short answers

o **Influence**

- Will provide longer answers
- May joke around
- May go off topic

o **Steadiness**

- Will solicit other opinions
- Will wait to be asked questions
- May be more quiet and reserved

o **Conscientiousness**

- Will take charge of taking minutes
- Likes getting to the point
- Will stick to the agenda

4. You can review the answers with your team.

Debriefing questions

- What do you now know about identifying DiSC styles that you did not know before?
- How will you use this exercise to help you communicate with different styles?

Identifying DiSC Styles

D	I
S	C

Identifying DiSC Styles

D	I
• Come prepared • Stick to business • Be clear • Get directly to the point	• Allow time for socializing • Ask them for their input • Provide them opportunities to be creative
S	**C**
• Give them time to make decisions • Ask specific questions • Be personal	• Present specifics • Create an action plan • Provide information to allow them to make an informed decision

What Does Your Desk Look Like... Honestly?

Purpose
To identify traits of each behavioural style.

Time/duration
15 minutes

Group size
Eight people, 15 people for the variation

Modality
Web conference - whiteboard

Materials
Use the template below for a variation of this exercise

Process
This exercise should only be done once the participants have an understanding of their own behavioural style.

- Divide the whiteboard into eight squares and assign a square to each person.

- Ask participants to draw an image of what their desk looks like right now.

- Ask each participant to explain their image.

Debriefing questions

- What traits did you notice about each style?

- What do you understand better about each style now that the activity is over?

- How does this help us understand how people work?

Variations

- Place the images seen below on a whiteboard.

- Have each participant choose the desk that closely resembles what their desk looks like.

Source

Graphics: http://search.creativecommons.org

What Does Your Desk Look Like... Honestly

CHAPTER 2

Getting to Know Each Other

Who are the people on our virtual team?

I'm Special

Purpose

Getting to know each other and determining what unique attributes each person brings to the team.

Time/duration

20 minutes

Group size

10 people

Modality

Teleconference

Materials

n/a

Process

At the beginning of the meeting ask each person to spend two minutes telling the team something unique about themselves as part of their introduction.

Examples:

- Culture
- Family
- Recreational activities
- Travel
- Skill set

Debriefing questions

- What did you learn about your team members?
- How does this exercise build team cohesion?

Match Box

Purpose

This exercise is for newly formed teams.

Getting to know about each other and to dispel assumptions about each other.

Time/duration

15 minutes

Group size

Eight-10 people

Modality

Web conference

Materials

PowerPoint slide with a picture of each team member on it.

Process

1. The facilitator asks each person to email a picture of themselves prior to the meeting.

2. The facilitator is to create a slide with the pictures and post the slide on the whiteboard.

3. Ensure that each picture is numbered.

4. The facilitator introduces the purpose of the exercise which is to match people's voices to their faces.

5. At the end of the meeting, the facilitator will choose one picture at a time and ask the team to guess who they think

it is using the raised hand feature, chat or by giving verbal responses.

6. Continue until all the voices and faces have been matched.

7. Ensure that everyone has the opportunity to participate.

Debriefing questions

• What did you notice about this exercise?

• What does that suggest to you about assumptions, and why?

• How might you use this as a result of this exercise?

Variations

If Web conferencing is not available send out the pictures ahead of time.

Colour Jacuzzi

Purpose
Getting to know each other.

Time/duration
15-20 minutes

Group size
15 people

Modality
Web conference – whiteboard

Materials
See slides below.

Process
1. Facilitator - recreate the slide shown below and post on a shared whiteboard.

2. Ask each person, one at a time, to answer the question next to the color they chose.

   - **Red** -The stop/danger color: what is the most thrilling thing you have ever done?

   - **Orange** -The motivation color: What motivates you?

   - **Yellow** - Creativity color: What is the best idea you ever had?

   - **Green** - Money color: What is the most outrageous thing you ever did with money?

- **Blue** - Sky's the limit color: What is your fantasy for the future?

- **Fuchsia** - An unusual color: What is the oddest thing you have ever seen?

- **Purple** - Color of royalty: If you were the ruler of the universe for one day what would be the 1st thing you would do?

Debriefing questions

- What did you learn about your colleagues that you did not know before?

- How did this exercise help you build trust with your team members?

Variations

Change colors to images such as:

- Animals

- Cloud formations

- Landscapes

Source

Unknown

COLOR Jacuzzi - Exercise

COLOR Jacuzzi - *choose one*

Red

Orange

Yellow

Green

Blue

Fuchsia

Purple

COLOR Jacuzzi – Exercise _{cont}

Red	The stop/danger color: what is the most thrilling thing you have ever done?
Orange	The motivation color: What motivates you?
Yellow	Creativity color: what is the best idea you ever had?
Green	Money color: What is the most outrageous thing you ever did with $$
Blue	Sky's the limit color: What is your fantasy for the future
Fuchsia	An unusual color: What is the oddest thing you have ever seen?
Purple	Color of royalty: Universe ruler for the day- the 1st thing you would do?

Facial Expressions

Purpose

Getting to know each other.

Time/duration

15 minutes

Group size

Maximum 15 people

Modality

Web conference - whiteboard

Teleconference

Materials

PowerPoint slide showing a variety of facial expressions

Process

Prerequisite:

Everyone on the team must have taken the DiSC behavioural assessment and reviewed the characteristics of each DiSC style.

Instructions:

1. Prepare a slide with a variety of facial expressions or use the sample provided.

2. Ensure there is at least one facial expression per person.

3. Begin by having each participant select a facial expression.

Have each participant share:

- What the facial expression reflects about themselves and,

- How it relates to their DiSC style.

Debriefing questions

- How does this help build team cohesion?

- What does this suggest to about this group/team?

Source

Starting up a Virtual Team by Stu Noble originally published in the February 2004 Issue of Link & Learn.

Facial Expression found through Creative Commons Search: http://search.creativecommons.org/

Facial Expressions

40

Getting to Know Me

Purpose

Getting to know each other.

Time/duration

20 minutes

Group size

Five-10 people

Modality

Web conference - whiteboard

Materials

Template shown below

Process

Have the facilitator create a grid (see sample below) on the whiteboard. Choose six questions from the list below. Have the participants answer each question using their writing tool.

- Were you named after anyone?

- What is your favorite food?

- Do you have kids?

- Do you use sarcasm?

- Do you have all your hair?

- Would you go parachuting?

- Do you untie your shoes when you take them off?

- What is your favorite flavour of ice cream?

- What is the first thing you notice about people?

- What do you consider to be one of your greatest attributes?

- What color shirt and shoes are you wearing?

- What was the last thing you ate?

- What distractions are there in your environment?

- What is your favorite smell?

- What is your favorite sport to watch?

- What is your hair color and eye color?

- What is the last movie you watched?

- What is your favorite season?

- What book are you reading now?

- What is on your mouse pad?

- What did you watch on television last night?

- What is the farthest you have been from home?

- Do you have a special talent?

- Where were you born?

Debriefing questions

- What struck you about the answers?

- What does this suggest to you about yourself and the group?

- How could you build on the information you learned today?

Variations

• At the beginning of each meeting have the facilitator choose one from the list above and ask each team member to respond.

• Prior to the meeting choose five-10 questions and distribute them to the team via email. Have the participants answer the questions and return them to the facilitator. Create a table with the questions and the answers and have the team members match the answers to the appropriate person.

Getting to Know Me

What is the first think you notice about people?	What do you consider to be one of your greatest attributes?
What distractions are there in your environment?	Where were you born?
Do you have a special talent?	What was the last thing you ate?

Across the Hall, Around the World

CHAPTER 3

Now That We Know Each Other

What else would be helpful to know about the people on our virtual team?

Peeling the Layers

Purpose

Gain a better understanding of how people like to work.

Time/duration

10-20 minutes

Group size

Five-10 people

Modality

Teleconference or web conference

Materials

n/a

Process

Have each person on the team share a personal idiosyncrasy that others should know in order to work more effectively together, for example:

- I get really annoyed when people interpret when someone else is speaking.

- It irritates me when people multi-task on a teleconference.

- I prefer that when someone disagrees with me they have supporting rational.

- I feel isolated working in my home office. It would be nice to hear from team members more frequently.

Debriefing questions

- What did you learn by listening to your colleagues?

- What does this suggest to you about yourself and the group?

- How are you going to use this information?

Source

Unknown

So Much in Common

Purpose

Demonstrate that people often have more in common than they initially might think they have.

Time/duration

40 minutes in total:

- Five minutes for instructions
- 15 minutes for the activity
- 10 minutes for the activity debrief
- 10 minutes to get in and out of break out rooms

Group size

Three people per breakout room

Modality

Breakout rooms (some teleconference and web conference suppliers have the ability to provide participants with "breakout rooms" where smaller groups within the whole group can work together and then come back together)

Materials

n/a

Process

1. Have the facilitator divide the group into teams of three people per breakout room.

2. Ask the team members to list 10-15 items that each of the three team members have in common.

3. They will have 15 minutes to complete this task.

4. Have the participants return to the main room to debrief the activity.

Debriefing questions

• What did you notice about this exercise?

• What were some of the unusual items you discovered?

• How did you uncover these areas of commonalities?

• What implications does this have for us as members of a virtual team?

Source

Adapted from *Even more Games Trainers Play-Experiential Learning Exercises* by Edward E. Scannell & John Newstrom (1994).

Who's in the Tank?

Purpose
To become better acquainted with each other.

Time/ duration
15 minutes

Group size
Four -10 people

Modality
Web conference

Materials
PowerPoint slide showing a variety of fish images (see sample below).

Process
Prerequisite:

- Ensure that team members have completed the DiSC assessment.

Instructions:

1. Prepare a slide with a variety of fish images or use the sample provided.
2. Begin by having each participant select a fish.

Have each participant share:

- What the fish reflects about themselves and,
- How it relates to their DiSC style.

Debriefing questions

- What did you notice about your colleagues' answers?

- How does this exercise help us to become better acquainted with each other?

- How does this help build team cohesion?

Source

Fish images found through Creative Commons Search: http://search.creativecommons.org/#.

Who's in the tank?

If I take my time and am goal orientated then I am a...	If I am aggressive and like to stick to facts then I am a...
C	D
If I take my time and am goal orientated then I am a...	If I am playful and fast moving then I am a...
S	i

A Penny for Your Thoughts

Purpose
Sharing past work experiences.

Time/duration
30 minutes

Group size
Maximum 15 people

Modality
Teleconference

Materials
Each participant brings a coin from his/her country to the meeting.

Process
Have the participants look at the year on their coins and then answer the following questions:

- Describe the job you were doing in that year.
- What skills did you learn then, that you are now bringing to this team?

Debrief questions
- What struck you about this exercise?
- How does this help you understand your team members better?

- What are the strengths of the team?
- Where are there gaps?

Variations

Have the participants describe a significant event in their lives or country in the year of the coin.

Dinner Date

Purpose
Getting to know about each other.

Time/duration
10-15 minutes

Group size
10-15 people

Modality
Teleconference

Materials
n/a

Process
Have each team member complete the following statement:

- "If I could have dinner with any person, living or dead, it would be _____. The reason is _____.

- Have each team member share their answers with the rest of the team.

Debriefing questions
- What did you learn about your team members?

- What similarities/differences did you notice about each statement?

- How does understanding similarities/differences contribute to building a stronger virtual team?

Variations

"If I could bring a person, dead or alive to work with us on this team it would be_____ because _____".

Across the Hall, Around the World

CHAPTER 4

Building Trust

I have never met the people on my team. How can we start to build a trusting relationship so that we can work together effectively?

Team Perceptions

Purpose

Building trust by generating a list of perceptions about virtual teams and to discuss how these perceptions can impact the productivity of a virtual team.

Time/duration

20 minutes

Group Size

10 participants

Modality

Web conference - whiteboard

Materials

n/a

Process

Prior to the meeting have the facilitator list the three perceptions on a whiteboard or use the sample below.

Choose a perception and discuss how it would impact the team if someone on your team believed this perception to be true.

Perceptions:

1. We can't trust people we have never met.

2. Virtual teams are easier to manage because people focus on work and not people.

3. The key to virtual team success is good electronic collaboration software.

Debriefing questions

- If you had someone on your team who believed these perceptions to be true how would you handle it-(go through each perception separately)?

- What can the team do to minimize the impact of these perceptions?

Variations

- Have the team members generate a list perceptions and determine how that belief would impact the team.

- Start off each meeting with a short discussion of one of the perceptions and how it impacts the team.

- (If using whiteboard, save finished document and email to participants).

Virtual Team Perceptions

What is the first think you notice about people?	What do you consider to be one of your greatest attributes?
What distractions are there in your environment?	Where were you born?
Do you have a special talent?	What was the last thing you ate?

The Gift of Positive Feedback

Purpose

To promote a climate of self-worth, positive reinforcement, trust and appreciation within a team.

Each team member will provide positive feedback to one other team member.

Time/duration

One minute per person

Group size

10-15 people

Modality

Web conference - chat feature

Materials

n/a

Process

Facilitator Notes:

1. In order to make this a more successful exercise, begin by talking about the value of giving feedback to team members.

2. There may be some participants who are uncomfortable receiving and giving feedback in front of others. Once you pair up the participants let them know that they can use private or public chat when providing their feedback.

3. Ensure participants have completed the DiSC assessment.

Instructions:

Pair up team members and instruct them to:

- Describe a strength or notable success of their partner
- Make the message specific to that individual
- Make the message personal by using the person's name
- Be genuine
- Begin your sentence with, "I like…", "I feel…", or "I think…"

Example:

"Joe, I like how you got everyone to participate on the last teleconference call."

Debriefing questions

- Which disc styles had the most difficulty giving feedback and why?
- How did you feel about receiving/giving this feedback?
- What did you learn from listening/observing your colleagues giving feedback?
- For some of you this exercise was outside of your comfort zone, why would it be important to do something which might feel uncomfortable?
- How would giving feedback contribute to building trust with your colleagues?

Source

Author unknown

Yes but…. Yes and….

Purpose

The goal of this exercise is to have the individual team members build on each others ideas.

Time/duration

15 minutes

Group size

15 people

Modality

Teleconference

Materials

n/a

Process

Assign a number to each team member, for example:

- One - Claire
- Two - Eric
- Three - Josh
- Four - Sam

Part one - Yes but...

1. Have team member number one make a statement about any topic.

2. Person number two responds with a sentence that begins with *"yes but..."*

3. Each person in turn responds to the previous person by beginning their sentence with **"yes but..."**

4. Continue this until each person has had several turns.

Example

- Team member one: "My dog is wonderful."

- Team member two: **"Yes but**... your dog has fleas."

- Team member three: **"Yes but**...I used Dr. Flea's flea wash to get rid of it."

- Team member four: **"Yes but**... he still smells bad."

Part two - Yes and...

1. Have team member number one make a statement about any topic.

2. Person number two responds with a sentence that begins with **"Yes and..."**

3. Each person in turn responds to the previous person by beginning their sentence with **"Yes and..."**

4. Continue this until each person has had several turns.

Example

- Team member one: "My dog is wonderful."

- Team member two: **"Yes and**... she is very obedient."

- Team member three: **"Yes and**.... she smells so great."

- Team member four: **"Yes and**.... I don't mind now when she sits on my lap."

Debriefing questions

Debrief for Yes but...

- How did this exercise make you feel?

- What parallels can you draw between this exercise and your real life?

- What could we have done differently?

Debrief for Yes and...

- How did this exercise make you feel?

- How was this exercise different from the yes but exercise?

- How did it impact you differently?

- How does building on each other's ideas impact trust?

Source

Second City Improv

It's in the Mail

Purpose

Building trust and team cohesiveness.

Time/duration

Two minutes per person

Maximum of two people during a two hour session

Group size

Maximum 20-25 people

Materials

See process below

Process

1. Prior to the session, have participants email one unique and unknown piece of information about themselves to the facilitator.

2. Have the facilitator read one of the emails to the group, either at the beginning of the session or during a lull.

3. Have the group guess who the owner of the information is.

4. Once the group guesses correctly, the owner may provide additional details.

Examples:

- Back up singer for Whitney Houston

- Spun themselves in a dryer

- Is a competitive ballroom dancer

- Have five grandchildren
- Won $800,000

Debriefing questions

- How does this exercise help you build team cohesiveness?
- How does this exercise help you build trust amongst your team members?

Variations

For the a face-to-face meeting:

1. Have participants write the unique piece of information on a slip of paper and deposit it in a cup. The participants are not to put their names on the slip of paper.

2. At the beginning of the session or when there is a lull in the energy, have a participant draw out a piece of paper and read it to the group.

3. Have the group guess who the owner of the information is.

4. Once the group guesses correctly, the owner may provide additional details.

Start a New Sentence

Purpose

The goal of this exercise is to have the individual team members build on each others ideas.

Time/duration

Five-10 minutes

Group size

Five-15 people

Modality

Teleconference or web conference

Materials

n/a

Process

1. Assign a number to each team member, for example:

   One - Claire

   Two - Susan

   Three - Josh

   Four - Eric

2. Have person number one make a statement about virtual teams (specific to their virtual team or virtual teams in general).

3. Have team member number two begin the next statement using the last word in the previous statement.

4. Team member number three begins their statement with the last word of the previous statement.

5. Continue until the facilitator says to stop.

Example:

- Team member one: "My virtual team has communication *challenges*."

- Team member two: "*Challenges* such as communication can impede *trust*."

- Team member three: "*Trust* is one of the most important factors in determining virtual team *success*."

- Team member four: "*Success*, according to many studies, is based on trust and collaboration."

Debriefing questions

- What happened?

- What did you find yourself listening to?

- Who had the same experience?

- Who reacted differently?

- What does that suggest to you about yourself and your team?

- What might we conclude from these observations?

- What actions might you take?

- When you build on each others' ideas how does that impact trust?

Facilitator note: Often we don't listen to everything the person says, or we just listen to what we think is relevant or important.

Source

Adapted from Second City Improv

CHAPTER 5

Building a Cohesive Team

How do others on the virtual team perceive me?

How do we build on each others ideas?

What can we share with each other that will improve our communication within the virtual team?

Stone Soup

Purpose

Create a story from the perspective of your DiSC style.

Time/duration

50 minutes:

- Five minutes for instructions
- 15 minutes for the activity
- 10 minutes for presentation
- 10 minutes for debrief
- 10 minutes to get in and out of break out rooms

Group size

12-15 people

Modality

Break out rooms (some teleconference and web conference suppliers have the ability to provide participants with break-out rooms where smaller groups within the whole group can work together and then come back together).

Materials

See picture below

Process

Facilitator:

- Show the Stone Soup picture and instruct the DiSC styles to create a story about the picture from the perspective of their DiSC styles.

- Divide the team into their dominant DiSC styles,

- Send the groups to their break out rooms,

- Have participants return to the main room,

- Each group presents their story to the rest of the team.

Note:

- The teams should have a minimum of two people per DiSC style. If one of the DiSC styles is not represented in the group ask people to volunteer to join that group.

Debriefing questions

- What did you notice about each story?

- What was different about each story?

- What was your reaction to the story?

- What does that tell us about each DiSC style?

- How would you apply this back at work?

Debriefing point

A successful team is a team where all four styles are represented. Each style brings strengths to the team.

D - brings directions and leadership

i - brings creativity

S - brings stability to the team

C - brings detail and order

Source

Ann McGovern

Picture by Winslow Pinney Pels

Create a story from the perspective of your DiSC styles

STONE SOUP

BY ANN McGOVERN • PICTURES BY WINSLOW PINNEY PELS

TV Commercial

Purpose

Create a commercial from the perspective of your DiSC styles.

Time/duration

50 minutes:

- Five minutes for instructions
- 15 minutes for the activity
- 10 minutes for presentation
- 10 minutes for debrief
- 10 minutes to get in and out of break out rooms

Group Size

10-15 people

Modality

Breakout rooms (some teleconference and web conference suppliers have the ability to provide participants with breakout rooms where smaller groups within the whole group can work together and then come back together).

Materials

n/a

Process

Facilitator:

1. Instruct the participants to create a 30 second commercial promoting their DiSC style.

2. Divide the team into their dominant DiSC styles.

3. Send the groups to their breakout rooms.

4. Bring the participants back to the main room.

5. Each group presents their commercial to the rest of the team.

Note:

The teams should have a minimum of two people per DiSC style.

Debriefing questions

• What did you find easy/difficult about working in your DiSC teams?

• What does that tell us about working with the same styles?

• What does each style bring to the team?

• How would you apply this back at work?

Debriefing point

A successful team is a team where all four styles are represented. Each style brings strengths to the team.

D - brings directions and leadership

i - brings creativity

S - brings stability to the team

C – brings detail and order

Variations

If breakout rooms are unavailable through your teleconference or web conference supplier have participants prepare the commercial prior to the session and present their commercial at the next meeting.

Source

Unknown

Who Needs Leadership Skills

Purpose

To determine the leadership skill requirements of a remote team member.

The goal of this exercise is to have the teams recognize that in a virtual team each member needs to rely on their leadership skills not just the skills of the leader.

Time/duration

40 minutes:

- Five minutes for instructions
- 15 minutes for the activity
- 10 minutes for debrief
- 10 minutes to get in and out of break out rooms

Group Size

10 people

Modality

Breakout rooms (some teleconference and web conference suppliers have the ability to provide participants with breakout rooms where smaller groups within the whole group can work together and then come back together).

Materials

n/a

Process

Divide the group into two teams:

Group one

1. Have the participants brainstorm a list of leadership skills and behavioural requirements of a remote leader.

   Possible answers: superior communication skills, technical proficiency, accessibility, organized, ability to facilitate meetings, coach, mentor and sensitivity to diversity.

Group two

1. Have the participants brainstorm a list of skill/behaviour requirements of a remote team member.

   Possible answers: accessibility, willingness to work together, strong communication skills, organized, commitment to the team and the goal.

Both groups

2. Send the groups to their breakout rooms.

3. Have the participants return to the main room to debrief the exercise.

Debriefing questions

- What was different about the lists?

- What was the same about the lists?

- Focus on the items that are the same-what conclusions can you draw from that?

- What can the leader and team member do to promote these skills?

Variations

If breakout rooms are unavailable through the teleconference or web conference supplier the activity, ask the participants to whiteboard their answers.

Healthy or Unhealthy

Purpose
Determine a definition of characteristics of a healthy team.

Time/duration
20 minutes

Group size
10 people

Materials
n/a

Modality
Web conference - whiteboard

Process
Facilitator:

1. Give participants two minutes to brainstorm a list of healthy characteristics of a virtual team.

2. Have participants transcribe their ideas onto the whiteboard.

3. Have participants elaborate on their ideas.

    o **Option one:**

    • Choose the top three that are current strengths of the team and brainstorm ways to cultivate them.

    o **Option two:**

- Choose the top one or two (depending on time) that the team would like to improve on and brainstorm ways to incorporate them onto your team.

Debrief questions

- What did you observe about this exercise?
- What does this activity suggest to you about healthy behaviours in general?

Source

Adapted from L. Thayer, "The Healthy Personality: Your Definition or Mine?" in L. Thayer (Ed.), *50 Strategies for Experiential Learning: Book Two*, University Associates, 1981.

One Word at a Time

Purpose

The goal of this exercise is to have the individual team members build on each others ideas.

Time/duration

20 minutes

Group size

Four-10 people

Modality

Teleconference

Materials

n/a

Process

Round One

This activity requires two volunteers who will create a story adding one word at a time. The rest of the participants will act as observers.

For example:

Topic-asking to a raise

- Team member one - "Dear"
- Team member two - "Boss,"
- Team member one - "I"

- Team member two - "would"
- Team member one - "like"
- Team member two - "a"
- Team member one - "raise."
- Team member two - "My"
- Team member one - "work"
- Team member two - "is"
- Team member one - "fantastic!"

Instructor's notes for Round Two

If you have 6 people or less on the teleconference everyone can participate in round two.

Assign a number to each team member to control the sequence of the activity and to ensure everyone has a chance to participate.

For example:

1. Susan = one
2. Eric = two
3. Amy = three

Round two

Round two includes six participants or less

Round three

Round three includes seven-10 participants.

If you have over seven participants have other participants observe the activity.

Debrief questions

o **Round one-debrief with the pairs who did the exercise**

- How was this experience?

- What did you notice?

o **Round one-debrief with the observers**

- What did you notice about the activity?

- What was your reaction to it?

o **Round two-debrief with the team member who did the exercise**

- How was this experience?

- What did you notice?

o **Round two-debrief with the observers**

- What did you notice that was different in round two?

- What was your reaction to it?

o **Round three-debrief for everyone**

- How does relate to being on a virtual team?

o **Facilitators Note**

- Lack of individual control of the outcome

- Lack of buy-in to the group process and the end result

Variations

Instead of a story, the partners can create a

1. Memo to a colleague

2. Memo to the president of the company

3. Memo to a stakeholder

4. Memo to another team member

5. Dear John letter

6. Letter requesting a promotion

Source

Second City-Improv

Pig Personality

Purpose

Team building and fun.

Time/duration

10 minutes

Group size

10-15 people

Modality

Web conference

Materials

Pig personality assessment and the template shown below

Process

1. Individually ask each person to draw a pig (ensure you are not offending any cultures prior to doing this exercise).

2. Direct the team members to the following website and have them do the assessment on-line during the meeting (it takes about minutes minutes to complete) Pig Personality website: http://drawapig.desktopcreatures.com/drawApig. asp Have each team member share their responses.

or

2. Ask for six volunteers to draw the pig on the whiteboard. Have everyone else draw a pig on a sheet of paper Read the description below.

Note: After the exercise is completed let the participants know that there is no validity to the results of this assessment.

Interpreting the Pig Personality Profile

* If the pig is drawn toward the top of the paper, you are a positive and optimistic person.

* If the pig is drawn towards the middle of the page, you are a realist.

* If the pig is drawn toward the bottom of the page, you are pessimistic and have a tendency to behave negatively.

* If the pig is facing left, you believe in tradition, are friendly, and remember dates and birthdays.

* If the picture is facing forward (towards you), you are direct, enjoy playing the devil's advocate, and neither fear nor avoid discussion.

* If the pig is facing right, you are innovative and active, but have netiher a sense of family, nor remember dates.

* If the pig is drawn with many details, you are analytical, cautious, and distrustful.

* If the pig is drawn with few details, you are emotional, naive, care little for detial, and take risks.

* If the pig is drawn with four legs showing, you are secure, stubborn, and stick to your ideals.

* If the pig is drawn with less than four legs showing, you are insecure, or are living through a period of major change.

* The larger the pig's ears you have drawn, the better listener you are.

* And last but not least... the longer the pig's tail you have drawn, the more satisfied you are with the quality of your sex life.

Debriefing questions

None – this is just for fun!

Source

Pig Personality website: http://drawapig.desktopcreatures.com/drawApig.asp

Author unknown.

Across the Hall, Around the World

Cultural Diversity

How does understanding the cultural of our team members help us appreciate their similarities and differences?

How do different cultures interpret metaphors and how it can affect our communication?

Metaphor Magic

Purpose

To determine how different cultures interpret metaphors and how it can affect our communication.

Time/duration

15 minutes

Group size

10 people

Modality

Web conference – whiteboard

Materials

n/a

Process

1. Have the team members come up with a list of words or phrases that have different interpretations or meanings.

2. Ask your team members to define what they think it means.

Debriefing questions

*   What was your reaction to this exercise?

*   What does this suggest to you about using metaphors in our speech?

*   How can you apply this?

Facilitator Note:

Even when two people think they can speak each other's language, the chance of error is high. Usages and contextual inferences may be completely different between cultures.

Similarities and Differences

Purpose

To determine how commonalities contribute to the team's success.

Time/duration

15 minutes

Group size

10 people

Modality

Web conference – whiteboard

Materials

PowerPoint slide

Process

1. Facilitator recreates the slide shown below and posts it on a shared whiteboard prior to the meeting.

2. Have the team brainstorm similarities and differences of work patterns.

For example:

- Time zones, how we make decisions, how we work, language and how we communicate.

- Have the team members list on the whiteboard how these similarities and differences contribute to the success of our team.

Debriefing questions

- How did you feel about this exercise?

- How do these similarities and differences contribute to the success of our team?

- What did you learn that you didn't know before?

Similarities	
Differences EMBRACING OUR DIFFERENCES	

Understanding Culture

Purpose

By understanding cultural aspects of the team members life, personal relationships can be developed, which will ultimately lead to a better team environment.

Time/duration

15 minutes

Group size

Eight people

Modality

Web conference - teleconference

Materials

n/a

Process

At the beginning of a meeting have team members share something that is important in their life outside of work.

Examples:

- Family – "my in-laws live with me"
- Hobbies – "I play the bag pipes"
- National Days – "We celebrate the Queen's birthday"

Debriefing questions

- What do you know now that you did not know before?

- What does this suggest to you about cultural diversity in general?

- How does understanding your team members' culture contribute to a better team environment?

Variations

- If there are more than eight people in the meeting ask for volunteers to share something that is important in their life outside of work.

- If there are more than eight people in the meeting spread the exercise over a few meetings.

Cultural Adaptation

Purpose
To increase awareness of how team members can adapt.

Time/duration
15 minutes

Group Size
10 people

Modality
Web conference – whiteboard

Materials
See slide below

Process
1. Facilitator recreates the slide shown below and posts it on a shared whiteboard prior to the meeting.

2. Facilitator asks the participants to brainstorm the solutions to each adaptation using their writing tool.

Possible solutions:

o **Time Zones**

   • Allow extra time for time zone differences.

   • Attempt to schedule meetings during work hours.

   • Rotate meeting times to share the burden of after-work hours.

o **Spoken**

- Avoid slang/colloquialisms/jargon/acronyms, metaphors.

- Use simple language.

- Avoid humour.

- Stick to the point.

- Confirm understanding by asking open-ended questions.

- Reiterate key points.

- Acknowledge/invite each individual to speak.

- Allow for "think time" between responses.

o **Written**

- Write from the receivers point of view.

- Be more descriptive.

- Use lists/points.

- Use follow-up emails for feedback.

Debriefing questions

- What was your reaction to this exercise?

- What would be the consequence of not adapting to different cultures?

- What will you do differently from now on?

Source

Author Unknown

Cultural Adaptation

Type of Adaption	Specific Behaviors
Time Zones	
Spoken Language	
Written Language	

Global Understanding

Purpose

To appreciate the cultural similarities and differences of the team members.

Time/duration

20 minutes

Group size

10 people

Modality

Web conference – whiteboard

Materials

PowerPoint slide with participants' graphics

Process

1. Prior to the meeting the facilitator requests from each team member one image that represents or reflects their culture.

2. Have each team member email that image prior to the meeting.

3. Facilitator prepares a slide with the images received.

4. Have each participant explain why they choose their image and what it means to them.

Debriefing questions

- What did you learn about your team members?

- What similarities/differences did you notice about each culture?

- How does understanding similarities/differences contribute to building a stronger virtual team?

- What will you do differently now that you might not have done before?

Variations

Use the images below

How We Work

1

2

3

4

5

6

7

8

9

CHAPTER 7

Meetings

How to conduct an effective virtual meeting.

How Has Your Week Been Going?

Purpose

To determine how people are feeling between meetings.

It can be work related or personal (if they choose).

Time/duration

15 minutes

Group size

10 people

Modality

Web-conference - whiteboard

Materials

Use a variety of graphics such as the examples shown below

Process

1. Have the facilitator place the numbered images on the whiteboard.

2. Ask each participant (or ask for volunteers) to choose a number/graphic and describe how their week has been going.

3. The exercise is finished once all the participants have answered the question.

Debriefing questions

- What does this suggest to you about building team cohesiveness?

- How does this exercise help us understand how people are feeling?

- What modifications can you make that will work for you?

Sources

Adapted from Tom Heck-Teach Me Teamwork

Source: http://search.creativecommons.org/

How's Your Week Been Going?

Meeting Bingo

Purpose
To gain a better understanding of the participants' preferences regarding virtual meetings.

Time/duration
15 minutes

Group size
8 people

Modality
Teleconference or web conference

Materials
Bingo card (see sample below)

Process
1. At the beginning of the meeting have the meeting facilitator or coordinator post the Bingo 'Card' (see attached sample), on the whiteboard.

2. Have each person check off two items that most applies to them. Facilitator asks each participant to explain why they chose those items.

Debriefing questions
• What does this tell us about our virtual meeting preferences?

• What will you do differently from now on?

Variations

Rewrite or add different items to customize the Meeting Bingo Card to the team.

Meeting Bingo

Likes the use of icebreakers	Likes the agenda distributed at least 48 hours prior to the meeting
Prefers morning meetings	Finds virtual meetings challenging
Prefers meetings Tuesday through Thursday	Likes to take on a role during the meeting, i.e. scribe, timekeeper and facilitator

There's a Pink Elephant in your Bathtub

Purpose
Often emails are not read between meetings. This exercise is a creative way of encouraging people to read their emails.

Time/duration
5 minutes

Group size
Unlimited

Modality
Teleconference or web conference

Materials
n/a

Process
1. Prior to the meeting have the meeting facilitator or coordinator send out a lengthy email to each team member. Embedded in this email will be the following statement: "there is a pink elephant in your bathtub."

2. In the meeting ask for volunteer(s) to summarize or identify the key points in the email.

3. The exercise is over when someone discovers the embedded statement.

Debriefing questions

- What did you notice?

- Why is this significant?

- What will you do differently from now on?

- Which DiSC style(s) is mostly likely/least likely to identify the embedded statement?

Variations

Have a quiz at the beginning or end of each meeting about the emails you have sent since the last meeting.

How Did We Do?

Purpose
To determine the effectiveness of the meeting.

Time/duration
10 minutes

Group size
Up to 10 people

Modality
Web conference – whiteboard

Materials
Template shown below

Process
This exercise is conducted at the end of the meeting.

1. Before the meeting prepare a gird as seen below. Assign a square to each individual.

2. At the end of the meeting ask each person to draw a picture of an animal that reflects how they felt about the meeting.

3. Have each person explain what their animal means to them.

Note: This exercise can be used instead of a formal feedback process.

Debriefing questions

- How did you feel about the exercise?

- What does that suggest to you about the importance of providing feedback for meetings? And why?

- What might you do differently as a result of this exercise?

Variations

If you are not using a web conference application you can ask each person to name the animal that reflects how they felt about the meeting.

How Did We Do?

Maria	Sajid	Josh
Sam	Heidi	Hans
Omar	Aziz	Eric

Across the Hall, Around the World

CHAPTER 8

Review Our Discussions

We've covered a number of topics during our virtual team meeting. What insights have we gained from our discussions?

Self Discovery

Purpose

To assist the participants in gaining insight about their behavioural traits based on the DiSC assessment.

To facilitate self-discovery.

To improve working relationships and communications by understanding ourselves before trying to understand others.

Time/duration

45 minutes:

- Five minutes for instructions
- 15 minutes for the activity
- 15 minutes for the debrief
- 10 minutes to get in and out of break out rooms

Group size

12-15 people

Modality

Breakout rooms (some teleconference and web conference suppliers have the ability to provide participants with breakout rooms where smaller groups within the whole group can work together and then come back together).

Materials

DiSC assessment for each participant

Copy of questions: see Item #4 in Process below

Process

1. Pre-work: the participants must have completed the DiSC assessment (15-20 minutes).

2. Have the facilitator assign partners to discuss the results of the assessment.

3. Send the pairs to their breakout rooms

4. Have the pairs answer the following questions:

   - Was the assessment accurate in your opinion?

   - What did you learn about yourself that you didn't know before?

   - What are two areas that you identified as your strengths?

   - How can you capitalize on them?

   - What are two areas of challenge that you would like to change?

   - What can you do in the immediate future to work on them?

   - What help do you need from your team members to overcome this challenge in the long term?

Debriefing questions

- What struck you about this exercise?

- How does this help you understand the strengths and the challenges you bring to the team?

- What will you do differently now that the activity is over?

Variation

Have the pairs discuss this prior to the session and debrief the results in the meeting.

Table of Junk

Purpose
Provide the team with an opportunity to review/reinforce the learnings of the session.

Time/duration
15 minutes

Group size
15 people

Modality
Web conference

Materials
PowerPoint slide with a variety of graphics (see sample below)

For example: mouse trap, timer, comb, lock, ball, roll of tape, magnifying glass, magnet, glue

Process
1. Prepare a slide with a variety of graphics (see sample below)

2. Ensure there is at least one graphic for each person.

3. Begin by having each participant select a graphic.

4. Give the group a minute to think about how the object connects to the topic of the session.

   For example, for the session topic "Cultural Diversity in Virtual Teams:"

   • **Graphic chosen:** magnifying glass

- • **Interpretation:** Sometimes we need to use a magnifying glass to view how our biases about other cultures impact the team.

5. Ask the participants to share their interpretations.

Debriefing questions

- • What stood out for you?
- • Why was it significant?
- • What does that suggest to you about _____ (topic name e.g. cultural diversity in virtual teams)?
- • What can we draw from that?

Variations

Use:

a. At the beginning of a session to initiate creative thinking.

b. At end of a session to help the team review their learning.

Table of Junk

1

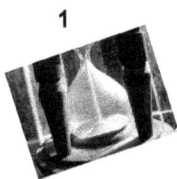

2

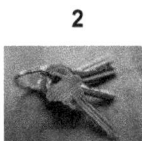

3

5

6

4

7

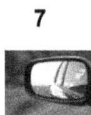

8

Vertical Word Association

Purpose
Reviewing the session's topic.

Time/duration
Five minutes

Group size
15 people

Modality
Web conference - whiteboard

Materials
PowerPoint slide with a word(s) vertically displayed

Select a team-related topic such as:

- Building teams
- Roles and responsibilities
- Building trust
- Team agreements
- Cultural diversity
- Managing expectations

Process

1. Have the participants write the word vertically down the centre of a piece of paper.

   If using a web conferencing tool, create a slide with the words placed vertically down the centre of the whiteboard.

2. For each letter, have the participants brainstorm a word or phrase that begins with that letter and is associated with the topic.

   Example: Topic - "Building Teams".

   B – bolster morale

   U – understanding other team members

   I – inclusive

   L - long-distance

   D – develop rapport

   I – interaction

   N - networking

   G – genuine

   T – trust

   E – enthusiastic

   A – accountable

   M – managing relationships

   S – stability

3. Ask for one or two volunteers to provide answers.

Debriefing questions

- This exercise is used as a debrief for a previous discussion.

119

Wheel of Fortune

Purpose

Reviewing key concepts from a previous session.

Time/duration

Five -15 minutes

Group size

15 people

Modality

Web conference/teleconference

Materials

Paper and pen if using teleconference

Process

1. The facilitator selects a two or three word concept from a previous meeting.

2. The facilitator gives direction to the participants, for example:

   • This concept has three words

   • The first word has three letters in it

   • The second word has five letters in it and

   • The third word has four letters in it

Example:

Concept: "Team Operating Agreement"

Have the participants fill in the blanks for each of the three words.

3. If using teleconference, instruct the participants to draw lines on a piece of paper based on the number of letters in each word.

4. If using the white board, prepare the puzzle prior to the session.

5. Participants will then ask the facilitator if a particular letter is in the word. If it is, the participants fill in that letter in the blank space on their sheet of paper.

6. The game ends when a person or a team has figured out the name of the concept.

Debriefing questions

• What stood out for you in this exercise?

• Why is this concept important for virtual teams?

DiSC-Covery

Purpose

To learn more about DiSC styles and how they contribute to building an effective virtual team.

Time/duration

15-20 minutes

Group size

10-15 people

Modality

Web conference

Materials

Chart with the questions and answers, shown below

Process

1. Ensure that the team has taken the DiSC assessment prior to this exercise.

2. Post the questions shown below onto a whiteboard.

3. Take a moment to review the questions on the whiteboard. When you have finished reading it please use your raised hand feature to indicate that you have finished reading it.

Facilitator note: ensure all hands are lowered before continuing on.

Now the competition begins:

4. When you think you know the answer to any of the questions, raise your hand.

5. The game ends when all the questions have been answered.

6. The person with the most points at the end of the game is the winner.

7. Review the answers with your team.

Questions:

1. What does D,i,S,C stand for?

2. Identify an important consideration when communicating with each style.

   D _____

   i _____

   S _____

   C _____

3. How does each style contribute to a balanced virtual team?

4. How might you identify or recognize each style on a web conference?

   D _____

   i _____

   S _____

   C _____

5. Which two styles are fast paced?

6. Which two styles are task oriented?

Answers:

1. What does D,i,S,C stand for?

   D-dominance

   i-influence

   S-steadiness

   C-Consciousness

2. Identify an important consideration when communicating with each style.

   D-be direct

   i-allow time for socializing

   S-show sincere interest in them

   C-provide them with facts and details

3. How does each style contribute to a balanced virtual team?

   D-provides leadership

   i-provides creativity

   S-provides stability

   C-provides structure

4. How might you identify or recognize each style on a web conference?

   D-will have a short direct answers

   i-will be animated

   S-will be more reserved

   C-will request details

5. Which two styles are fast paced?

   1. Dominance

   2. Influence

3. Which two styles are task oriented?

   1. Dominance

   2. Consciousness

Debriefing questions

- What did you observe?

- What can you conclude from these observations?

- How does an understanding DiSC style contribute to building an effective virtual team?

DiSC-Covery Questions

What does D,i,S,C stand for?	Identify an important consideration when communicating with each style	How does each style contribute to a balanced virtual team?
How might you identify or recognize each style on a web conference?	Which two styles are fast paced?	Which two styles are task oriented?

DiSC-Covery Answers

D-dominance i-influence S-steadiness C-Consciousness	D-be direct i-allow time for socializing S-show sincere interest in them C-provide them with facts and details	D-provides leadership i-provides creativity S-provides stability C-provides structure
D-will have a short direct answers i-will be animated S-will be more reserved C-will request details	1. Dominance 2. influence	1. Dominance 2. Consciousness

About the Authors

Susan Garms

Susan is a Senior Manager
in Telework and Change
Management Solutions within the
telecommunications industry. Susan
brings extensive expertise to her
clients, assisting them in achieving
balance on the people side of technical projects. She has
facilitated highly rated workshops for both remote workers and
their managers. Susan has experience and expertise as a remote
work specialist and has worked from her home in Richmond
Hill since 2000.

As a telework expert, Susan offers support through a
comprehensive, proven approach – from evaluation
to implementation to ongoing management, helping
organizations achieve their objectives. She also partners with
leading solution specialists on the design and implementation
of the technological infrastructure required for telework or
a more comprehensive virtual office solution for a mobile
workforce.

Susan has taken part in various conferences and seminars aimed at creating awareness of the issues and benefits of telework and its impact on individuals and organizations, including 2008's Saskatchewan Economic Development Association Conference, 2007's International Telework Symposium in Tokyo, various seminars for the Federated Press and Smart Commute in Ontario. She is a board member of the Canadian Telework Association and has her Change Management Certification from Prosci and the Change Management Learning Centre. Susan has worked in collaboration with VTB on various initiatives including this book.

Claire Sookman

Distinguished as Canada's pioneer in virtual team building, she specializes in helping teams that are geographically dispersed reduce their costs and reach their maximum potential, through training, coaching consulting and designing.

As the driving force behind the training/consulting firm of Virtual Team Builders, Claire Sookman brings to the table over a decade's worth of corporate training experience, working with well over 4,500 Managers in the past three years alone Specializing in virtual team building and communication strategies, Claire's company provides training that enables global teams to work more efficiently and effectively.

Claire's personalized, focused seminars have garnered numerous accolades, putting her services in high demand Worldwide. Some of her clients include: AT&T, Weyerhaeuser, CIBC, TD/ Canada Trust, Siemens, Bell Canada, Ministry of Correctional Services, USDA Forest Services, Sick Kids, Orange FT and GlaxoSmithKline.

In addition to acting as a consultant and trainer, Claire has participated in a range of public speaking conferences including: Project World, Seminars World, CEPEX, Federated Press, Institute for International Research, Human Resource Professional Association and McMaster's World Congress. In addition, Claire's articles have been published in CIO magazine, Computer World, Network World and in the Training Report. Claire is also a published author on Virtual Teams.

Claire's Products and Services helps organizations reduce costs and teaches global teams to work more effectively together.

Her polished communication and training skills were honed though both practical and educational channels including a Master Trainer Certification through Langevin learning Services. Claire's technical expertise in training is complimented by the Canadian Association for Professional Speakers and a long-standing association with Toastmasters International. Visit our website at www.virtualteambuilders. com. Take a minute to complete our Virtual Team Builders Needs Assessment and get a 5% discount on your next engagement with Virtual Team Builders. We look forward to being of assistance!

We hope you have enjoyed this book. We are always interested in learning what other people are doing that has worked for them. Feel free to send us your teambuilding activities, or best practices to info@virtualteambuilders.com.

Be sure to give us the source of your suggestions in order to give appropriate credit where due.

To Book Claire Sookman at your next convention, AGM or association meeting, contact:

info@virtualteambuilders.com

or

call 1-866-497-7749

To order Claire Sookman's & Susan Garms' books, CDs and other products please send an email to:

info@virtualteambuilders.com

Did you like this book?

If you enjoyed this book, you will find more interesting books at

www.MMPubs.com

Please take the time to let us know how you liked this book. Even short reviews of 2-3 sentences can be helpful and may be used in our marketing materials. If you take the time to post a review for this book on Amazon.com, let us know when the review is posted and you will receive a free audiobook or ebook from our catalog. Simply email the link to the review once it is live on Amazon.com, with your name, and your mailing address—send the email to orders@mmpubs. com with the subject line "Book Review Posted on Amazon."

If you have questions about this book, our customer loyalty program, or our review rewards program, please contact us at info@mmpubs.com.

Multi-Media
P u b l i c a t i o n s Inc.

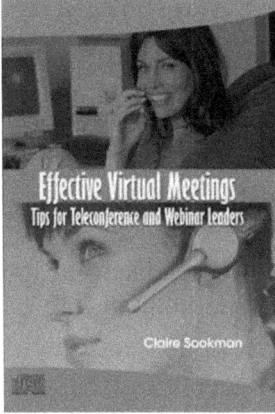

Effective Virtual Meetings: Tips for Teleconference and Webinar Leaders

Virtual team meetings (teleconferences, webinars, video conferences, etc.) are increasing in popularity as organizations look for ways to decrease costs and increase productivity, service delivery, and employee well being. Virtual meetings can be as effective as face-to-face meetings, at only a fraction of the cost; however, the effectiveness of these meetings is constantly threatened – 70% of participants in teleconferences and other virtual team meetings admit to being distracted during the events by other work activities.

This audio recording of an interview with Claire Sookman, a leading expert for over 15 years on virtual team management, reveals solutions to many common virtual team problems.

ISBN: 9781554890378   (Audio CD)
ISBN: 9781554890248   (MP3 Audio)

http://www.mmpubs.com/

www.ingramcontent.com/pod-product-compliance
Lightning Source LLC
Chambersburg PA
CBHW070406200326
41518CB00011B/2088